one little thing

Wendy,
Enjoy the
road trip!
♡ Stan Joy

one little thing: how to make big leaps with tiny steps

Printed in the United States of America. First printing 2012

Cover and interior design: Vanessa Perez

ISBN 978-0-9851140-0-8

For permission requests, write the publisher at the address below or the email address. Requests for quantity discounts and speaking engagement should be made via email to JMRDistributionPublishing@gmail.com

JMR Distribution Publishing
4120 Douglas Blvd #306—478
Granite Bay, CA 95746

how to make big leaps with tiny steps

one little thing

StaciJoy

CHAPTER ONE

If you can move your fork, you can transform your life.

People make things better because:

1. they want a better life
2. they are in CRISIS

Which do you prefer?

This is a book about getting healthy and staying healthy. I am not another healthcare practitioner who will lecture you on a complicated regimen of supplements and new habits to add to your life. Thinking you need to start an entirely different lifestyle may overwhelm and defeat you. No, I am here to tell you that changing ***one little thing*** can transform your life forever.

It's no mystery why one-third of Americans is obese and another third is overweight.[1] We do not move our bodies enough. We are stressed out. We eat too many calories but are grossly undernourished.

About 59% of adults do not exercise at all, according to Centers for Disease Control and Prevention.[2] The American Diabetic Association tells us that more than 20 million children and adults have diabetes.[3] Obesity is making millions of people sick and even killing them.

Forget about how we got here. Just look at where **you** are now and then decide where you want to be.

Reaching a goal is never as important as who you become along the way. You realize your dreams by making changes you can succeed at doing. Be selective about what you alter in your life.

Having the discipline to make your dreams come true can feel impossible. So tell yourself right now that you don't have to be a super-focused achiever if that doesn't feel like who you are. Getting from where you are to where you want to go requires you to develop a simple habit. If followed consistently, altering ***one little thing*** at a time will add up to the big things. This is the secret to creating what you want. It will change your life forever.

It's not always easy to make lifelong changes overnight. First, you must train your brain to accept the change process. Are you ready? This is easier than you might think.

TRY THIS:

A simple step to learn that change is easy

Make an easy change to something you have no emotional attachment to doing. Don't start with a change that feels like a sacrifice.

Every time you set your table, put the fork on the opposite side of your plate than the side where you usually place it.

Keep doing your new fork placement at every meal for one week. Even if you tell yourself that it's not important to keep your new table setting habit, do it anyway. This is how you learn to succeed at change. Do the new habit even when your mind tells you it doesn't matter. Just do it. It's not any extra effort to set the table a little differently. By doing it, you show yourself how easy change can be for you.

This action may seem pointless, but it actually trains your brain to make changes—an easy step with no downside and the huge upside of getting your brain ready to change your life.

After a week of your opposite fork placement, you are ready to make another change that requires something that may have an emotional attachment.

TRY THIS:

This time, make an easy change that might be a little harder emotionally.

For one week, switch to the opposite side of the bed than you are used to sleeping on.

There are very good reasons for making this change. First, it trains your brain to do something different as you hold the pattern. Second, if you have a partner, it elicits his or her cooperation and support in your process.

Fear the road to your healthy place?

Mike, an overweight, forty-something office manager, needed to lose 50 pounds. He had early signs of insulin resistance, high cholesterol, high blood pressure, and heart disease. Every day he led his team through action steps to achieve company goals. He knew what he was doing. He felt confident and he was a good leader. At the office, he had it nailed. But Mike was not feeling the least bit confident about his health. He expressed concerns about meeting personal health goals because every time he started to make healthy changes, he slipped off the road away from his destination. This normal pattern inevitably ended in self-doubt and discouragement. He was so worried about his failures at living healthier, what those failures meant, and what other people thought of him, that he was anxious and pessimistic about starting yet another failed journey toward good health.

Does Mike's story feel familiar?

Accept that you will lose your way and stray from the path from time to time.

This is normal. Think of your good health as your destination. It's where you want to be. It's what you're steering toward.

Program your health destination into your GPS navigational system.

The GPS does not care where you have been.

Your GPS doesn't care about how many U-turns you've had to make to get to this point. It doesn't even care if you've been driving in the opposite direction for the past 30 minutes, or even 30 years! The only thing your GPS cares about is getting you from where you are at this exact moment to where you told it you want to go.

What can you do when you feel yourself deviating away from your route?

RECALCULATE ROUTE!

Allow your internal GPS to choose an alternate route from where you are right now. It will get you there, but it will require you to know where you want to go, and find the best way from your current location.

RECALCULATE ROUTE is the most important phrase you can add to your health vocabulary. It's a soft and gentle response that doesn't make you beat yourself up or decide you've failed.

You would probably never put up with someone else treating you the way you treat yourself during a personal relapse. Lighten up on yourself. Stepping off course is a normal part of the journey—have faith in the process. Simply

RECALCULATE ROUTE and move on. It's a beautiful journey if you choose to see it that way.

The first step in any health restoration program is to figure out where you want to go.

Be realistic. You can't drive from Paris to New York. But you can drive from Paris to London. Be brave but reasonable when programming your destination to avoid recalculating your route too many times. Once you've decided where you want to be, it's OK to make some stops along the way to visit friends, or even special restaurants.

You are on a journey.

Where is your destination?

What is your desired outcome?

Do you want to shed 15 pounds?

Do you want more energy?

Do you want to reverse your diabetes?

Do you want more peace in your life?

Do you want to be profoundly happy?

Do you want to live a plant-based lifestyle?

Spend quality time choosing your goal before taking the next step. This is where you'll program your GPS to take you where you want to go. Take your time with this step because what you write will determine everything you do from this point forward.

Write your destination(s) in the space provided below.

Once you know your destination, knowing your "why" for getting there will help keep you on the road to success.

"Die" is a three-letter word in "DIET."

Stay away from diets.

Health experts say that 95% of all diets fail. This is not exactly true. Diets are successful because they are designed to take weight off. Where the sense of failure lies is in the fact that typically, people who are going on a diet are not equipped with the tools to maintain the same set of behaviors over an extended period of time that allowed them to take the weight off in the first place.

Diets do NOT fail. People fail. Expectations fail. You missed the turn—you failed. Big deal!

RECALCULATE ROUTE.

Most of us have tried and failed at countless diets. Diets are a radical message to your body that your body is going into deprivation and perhaps even starvation. This creates a psychological tug of war between what you tell yourself is acceptable to eat and what your mind obsesses over wanting to eat.

TRY THIS:

Get rid of a source of blame and shame in your journey to your health goals.

1. Walk over to your scale and pick it up.
2. Carry the scale in your arms as you walk up to the top floor of your home or building.
3. Open the window.
4. Make sure nobody is under the window.
5. Throw your scale out the window.

Don't forget to hike down to the sidewalk and clean up the mess! You don't need a metallic contraption frustrating and depressing you daily and even hourly with minor fluctuations in weight from water retention or muscle mass gain. Frequently getting on a scale can hurt your efforts to get healthy.

This book is designed to give you the tools you need to evolve into better health and stay healthy, whether you need to lose weight or reverse a disease process. If you want to run the marathon or play your sport without trashing your body, this book is for you. If you want to maintain consistent energy so you can go out there and live your life out loud with passion, purpose, and clarity, this is your trusted tool, your guide—the GPS for getting you there and keeping you there.

This book is about how to make big change easy. Are you tired of life's complexities? Complicated is not sexy. You're busy, you're in a hurry, and you need simple—you need easy. You need health. You need happiness. You need ***one little thing***.

Believe that you can do it!

In my nursing practice, I treated a young woman named Mary who was the mother of several small kids and was also struggling with a relatively new diagnosis of multiple sclerosis (MS). MS is an autoimmune disorder that affects mostly women and causes the myelin sheath around the axon structure in the nervous system to break down because of high levels of oxidative stress. In simple terms, her nervous system was operating slowly and ineffectively. Her symptoms were classic and included pain, tingling and numbness in the legs, blurred vision, and poor sleep patterns. She self-administered painful intramuscular injections to lessen the symptoms, but the shots caused bruising all over her legs.

Mary's diet was unhealthy by anyone's standards. She ate mostly processed foods filled with sugar, animal and trans/factory fats, and chemicals. Her life lacked whole food and fresh fruits and vegetables. It was obvious to both of us that nutrition was the area in which she needed to focus, but the first thing she said to me was, "Please don't make me give up my junk food. I'm perfectly happy right where I am."

I assured her that I wasn't going to take anything away from her. Since she had already experienced an enormous amount of loss simply trying to cope with her MS diagnosis, I wasn't interested in sinking her further into a sea of deprivation. That never works. I was simply going to give her the option to add ***one little thing*** to her life—just one thing.

One thing!

Not two things.

Not three things.

Mary chose to make her ***one little thing*** the simple act of adding whole food supplements, which are concentrated juice powders of fruits and vegetables, to her diet every day without fail. By adding so much nutrition in supplement form, Mary would benefit from the nutrients her body was crying for without feeling stressed about changing the eating habits that emotionally comforted her. She was instructed NOT to do anything else differently for at least four months. Her journey began in January, a hopeful way to begin a fresh new year.

In May, four months later, after staying consistent with her supplementation, Mary noticed subtle changes taking place within her body. She began to crave different kinds of foods, like more green vegetables and healthy smoothies. She found it interesting that some of her original cravings for sugar, saturated animal fats, and hydrogenated or trans/ factory fats began to melt away. The process felt completely natural to her.

On her own, Mary got to the place where she was ready to change another ***one little thing***. She chose to add a regular regimen of walking to her life. Four days a week, she briskly walked two miles when her husband was home to watch the children. She began to feel more energy in the morning as well as during her usual afternoon lull. She was beginning to really feel the magic of ***one little thing***.

Four months later, after consistently eating whole food concentrates and walking four days a week, Mary was ready to add another ***one little thing*** to her life. Since she felt so successful after adding whole food supplementation to her diet, she decided that examining her eating habits was the logical next step, even though the idea of changing her nutrition had been the most threatening thing to her when she first started the ***one little thing*** program. She decided to add two servings of fresh vegetables to her diet every day for the next four months. By developing the habit of eating two more green vegetables every day, she naturally expanded her repertoire of new vegetables to try, adding variety and nutritional synergy to her life when it was combined with the whole food supplement that was already a part of her daily routine.

Exactly one year from the time Mary began her health journey with the ***one little thing*** program, she noticed that her MS symptoms were diminishing. To their mutual amazement, she and her doctor agreed that she didn't need so many of her injection medications anymore. It worked. In one short year of taking consistent baby steps forward, Mary was able to travel with her family and live pain- and medication-free. Several years have passed and she now eats a very healthy, natural diet with little sugar or processed food, engages in consistent physical activity, and serves as a role model and an inspiration to her friends and family members.

Mary expressed to me during our initial consultation that she didn't want to spend the rest of her life on MS medications. She was afraid of her future. She was sliding down a slippery slope, experiencing symptoms that were becoming worse year after year. She wanted the joy of traveling with her family abroad. She wanted the stamina to live an active life and fully participate in activities with her busy, energetic children.

We typed these emotional "whys" in big, bold print, attached to them pictures of a woman playing with kids and families traveling to exotic destinations, and she hung them up on her wall to look at every day. She was clear about her destination.

Mary was successful because she accessed her reasons for changing. Her own emotional "why" had served as her internal inspiration button that she pressed whenever she felt herself on the wrong road. Mary used the RECALCULATING ROUTE principle on numerous occasions along the way. By slowly adding ***one little thing*** at a time, Mary discovered her personal path to health and energy. If someone with MS can turn her health around and live an active life by just changing ***one little thing***, imagine what you can accomplish.

What are the reasons why you desire your goals?

What emotions fuel them?

Do you want to experience the joy of playing on the floor with your kids or grandkids without pain?

Do you desire to lose your belly fat in six months so you can get a date to avoid loneliness?

Are you afraid that you will not live long enough to dance at your child's wedding in ten years?

Do you want to get in shape to avoid the humiliation of being teased by your friends when you can't make it to the top of Yosemite's Half Dome next spring?

Do you want to stop making excuses for the things you don't do?

Do you want to stop making excuses for the life you haven't led?

Write down your own "whys" in the space below. What are the emotions behind your dreams?

____

____

____

____

____

____

____

____

____

Now that you're connected to your personal destination, and have a "why" for taking the actions in this book, are you ready to learn more about your ***one little thing***?

CHAPTER TWO

Can you walk this far?

Movement

Heart disease is the leading cause of death for both men and women in America.[4] More than a third of heart attacks can be avoided by regular aerobic activity, yet only a third of Americans exercise regularly.[5] Humans have become sedentary beings, and women are even less active than men.

Is it time to RECALCULATE ROUTE?

This chapter is for those who desire to exercise, but don't know how to move past their mental barriers to doing it. Don't pressure yourself any longer to change your life. Just consider adding ***one little thing***.

For many people, just the thought of straining their bodies causes stress. They become distracted. They feel deprived. They feel discouraged by the constant starting and stopping of exercise programs. Eventually, they may feel that trying to change is no longer worth the mental anguish, and the idea of movement gets put on the shelf for awhile. Before they know it, a year goes by. They are still inactive, holding the notion that regular exercise is a possibility. Are they lazy? Are they frustrated? Are they disgusted? What is your story?

Choose ***one little thing***. Make the next course adjustment—just one. Stay with it for four months, or longer if you need more time. Don't you DARE do a thing more. If you try to do more than ***one little thing***, you'll cheat yourself and the entire system. Give this process a chance. Try to do things correctly. After four months, consider the option of choosing another ***one little thing***... or NOT. The decision is always yours to make every step of the way.

Some of you will need to choose an activity that supports your re-entry into the movement world and the activity will seem rudimentary or even a little bit stupid. The idea is to just get moving in the right direction.

Ignite your engine. Put it in forward drive. Allow yourself to become inspired by your own effort.

Find a buddy. Create your own personal cheerleaders in your partner, your spouse, your children, or your friends. When you elicit the support of others, you create the conditions to hold yourself accountable to the one commitment you've made to yourself. The social pressure you invite in will help keep you on the road to your destination.

Other readers may already be operating on a more advanced level when it comes to physical fitness. They may choose a more sophisticated ***one little thing*** that supports where they are today…or not. They may simply want to use the ***one little thing*** program to improve their attitude or nutritional status.

Is your ***one little thing*** running three miles every other day, or spending two hours in the gym five days a week? You'll know what you need. But more important, you'll know what course adjustment you have to make and that you're certain of doing. Follow your intuition. Choose the appropriate one activity for YOU and apply the ***one little thing*** principle.

TRY THIS:

WALK.

Add a WALK to your daily routine. Go out and buy new sneakers if you don't have good walking shoes. Get a cute exercise outfit if that's important to you and gets you excited to exercise. Or put on comfortable sweats and a T-shirt, if that seems easier. As far as your internal compass is concerned, the preliminary steps are not important. Just WALK. Put one foot in front of the other and walk from Point A to Point B.

Begin by adding at least 2,000 additional steps to your week. If you think that wearing a step counter on your wrist will help, purchase the widget. It doesn't matter if you walk slowly or if you walk briskly. It doesn't matter if you walk the dog, walk the stroller, or walk the treadmill. Just WALK. The idea is to simply get moving. You'll get so good at walking, and will feel so great doing it, that you'll want to walk for the rest of your life.

Walking may change your life.

Rachel suffered a heart attack at age 68. The first thing she did after her heart attack was give up smoking. Despite her step toward being healthier, Rachel gained a lot of weight the first year after giving up cigarettes. Rachel also suffered from arthritis, which caused her more pain when she tried to exercise. Her obesity and sedentary lifestyle put her in a high-risk category for developing disease.

Rachel was eventually diagnosed with cancer. After exploratory surgery was performed, Rachel was told by her oncology surgeon that the cancer had spread throughout her body and to get her affairs in order because he didn't expect her to live more than four months. She wanted to LIVE to see her children and her grandchildren grow into adulthood.

Rachel decided to change ***one little thing***: her attitude. This was not little. This was BIG. She decided that she was going to be the one to determine her own life expectancy. She chose to maintain a positive mental attitude, to ignore her arthritis pain for the moment, and to show gratitude for everything she had in life—her four adult children, her seven grandchildren, her beautiful home in the San Francisco Bay Area, and the consistent beating of her heart.

Rachel changed another ***one little thing***. Despite her arthritis pain, she started to walk. She committed to walking in a pattern around her suburban home once a day. She felt too fat and too frail to do anything else. For the first several weeks, it was once around the house. Then it was twice. Then it was a few times.

Four months later, Rachel made an unwavering commitment to her nutritional habits. She added whole food supplementation to her diet every day and made whole food, or unprocessed foods grown from the ground, the majority of her calories.

Rachel's ***one little thing*** was, "I'm going to walk around the house every day." This decision changed the direction of her journey forever. One year later, Rachel was no longer experiencing joint pain, and she walked five miles around a community lake near her home almost every day. In the process, she got out of her house and made friends. Rachel lost more than 40 pounds and she added seven more years to her life. She was delighted to spend time with her grandchildren as they grew. She was happy.

Live out loud. Speak your mind. Sing the music. Wear purple. Go with a friend. Walk in nature or a park if you can. Make it fun. Make it a desirable habit. Make it count.

But do not just focus on the final destination. Focus on the next turn you need to make to adjust your course… focus on that ***one little thing***.

Walking briskly can burn up to 350 calories per hour. Since it can take 3,500 calories to lose a pound, you could expect to lose a pound for every ten hours you walk, if you did nothing else. While this is true, don't pressure yourself to go from zero to hero overnight. Start slowly and work up to it. If you haven't been exercising, you can make your ***one little thing*** to add walking into your normal routine.

Park far away from the building and WALK it. Use your judgment and be safe. Don't park far away from the building if you know that you'll have to walk back to your car alone at night. Be sensible and be smart.

Where can you walk that you would normally drive? Instead of driving, WALK to the market around the corner, or to take your children to school. This may sound like a new concept to people who live in the suburbs or in a city like Los Angeles where people don't usually walk for daily errands. But if you haven't been exercising, be creative about walking more in your daily routine and do it consistently.

Try this for four months. Make regular entries in your calendar to walk for 10 minutes 4 days every week, and honor those times. You can do it for 10 minutes. Just get moving. Do not change ANYTHING else. You may want to, but resist the temptation.

This ***one little thing*** of walking might seem stupid and simple, but trust your internal compass. Do it for 16 weeks and see how you feel. Then, you can choose another ***one little thing***... or NOT. The choice is yours to make, every step of the way. Keep the pressure off yourself and make the process simple and positive.

Disclaimer: Some of you might have health issues that require medical supervision, such as heart disease or structural difficulties. Make sure to discuss with your doctor the plan to add more walking to your life. Please be safe and sensible about this.

Check in—Do you feel discouraged because four months seems too long? How about 16 weeks? If 16 weeks seems unbearable, consider 120 days. Ah, that sounds easier.

As a 17-year-old pre-nursing major at UCLA, I was thrown together with pre-medicine majors in difficult chemistry, physiology, and biology classes. I remember feeling mortified about having to enter the bell curve alongside intellects boasting 4.5 high school grade point averages. I quickly learned that I could handle anything for a 10-week quarter. The overwhelming anxiety of looking up at the top of the mountain from the bottom soon dissipated when I learned to RECALCULATE ROUTE. I learned to restructure my thought patterns around 10-week blocks of time.

When I failed my first college midterm, I felt devastated. I was ready to pack my bags and run back to the safety of home. But I held on to the notion that I could tolerate anything for 10 short weeks. I focused on putting one foot in front of the other for each 10-week period. I took on each day and each test. I conquered each class this way. Not only did I continue to pull myself out of my funk, but I eventually learned how to pull up my grades *and* my big-girl pants.

TRY THIS:

Here is another ***one little thing*** if you're ready after your four months of walking more…or NOT. Any change you make is your call.

Add 20 PUSHUPS and a ONE-MINUTE PLANK to your day, every day. It doesn't matter if you do straight-legged pushups or knees-on-the-floor pushups. This simple routine will add lean muscle mass to your arms and core muscle groups. Then, if you fall one day, your upper body will not be so weak that you won't be able to get up again. None of us wants to be helpless on the ground, crying, "I've fallen and I can't get up! Where is my emergency button necklace?"

If you can't do 20 pushups, do them until you literally cannot do one more, then try again the next day. You'll eventually be able to do 20 pushups. Practice the bent-arm plank every day until you can hold the position for one full minute.

This is what a plank looks like: Make your body straight and stiff as a wooden plank. The only two things that should be touching the floor are your bent toes and your forearms, bent at a 90-degree angle. Look down at the floor and loosen your neck muscles. Pull in and tighten your abdominal muscles, remember to breathe, and hold that pose for one full minute. It sounds easy, but it's not.

Practice both of these exercises for the rest of your life and feel your body change over time.

TRY THIS:

When you're ready for another ***one little thing***, consider adding one movement modality to your life one at a time…or NOT. You are the driver of the bus.

Choose ***one little thing*** from a list of activities such as swimming, cycling, regular yoga or hot Bikram yoga, Pilates, gym workouts, the Daily Method, interval training, an exercise boot camp, strength training, or training with a mobile fitness professional who will come to your home or your place of employment. After you've decided what ***one little thing*** will work best for you, work it into your calendar at least four days a week for 120 days and see what happens.

Maintaining regular movement is a challenge for many people. Acknowledge this and be kind to yourself.

Remember, you can always RECALCULATE ROUTE if you take the leap forward and swerve off course. Be proud of yourself for setting the goal to take your body back.

The desire is there. The drive is there. The destination is in place. You can change just ***one little thing***. The rest of the equation is up to you. See what you can accomplish in 120 days...or NOT.

CHAPTER THREE

How to handle stress before you're toast.

Attitude

Do you ever feel as though you're circling around the racetrack at 160 miles an hour, struggling not to let the potholes in the road spin you into a crash?

Do you sometimes feel like you're missing your turns, causing you to travel through your day apologizing to everyone for being late?

All of us feel stressed at times. In fact, 44% of people surveyed in an American Psychological Association study report that their stress has increased over the past five years.[6] What's more, 69% of us say we're stressed at our jobs.[7] One-sixth of workers stated that their stress at work makes them feel "angry enough to hit a coworker," reports *The Everything Stress Management Book*.[8]

Stress is dangerous. It takes a huge toll on our lives.

Stress affects us physically. A full 44% of people maintain that stress makes them feel unusually tired.[9] But that doesn't mean we sleep more, because 44% also report lying awake at night worrying.[10]

The way we handle stress can make us feel even worse. To cope with stress, 39% of people admit that they eat unhealthy food. Another 29% sometimes skip meals because of stress.[11]

It affects us emotionally. Studies show that 60% of the people say stress plagues them with feelings of irritability or anger.[12] The emotional strain can be hard to bear, which is why one-quarter of all women in the U.S. have been prescribed a drug for mental health issues such as depression and anxiety.[13]

Stress also contributes to the development of alcoholism, obesity, suicide, drug addiction, cigarette addiction, and other acts that cripple our health, and can even cause death.

Stress is hurting us.

It's even killing some of us.

News flash: The stress is never going to go away.

It's time to RECALCULATE ROUTE.

The important thing to remember is that we do not have control over most of the stressful stimuli that fly at us.

Do you remember the driver's education simulator machine designed to show students the unpredictable dangers of driving a car? Think of driving in the simulator, managing the endless distractions that challenge you—the ball rolling into the street, the child who runs out in front of you, or the dog that suddenly appears, causing you to swerve out of the way.

You are the simulator driver.

The road conditions are always going to be unpredictable whether you want them to be or not. Accept that obstacles will constantly appear in your path. How can you be ready to make the necessary adjustments? How can you reduce your feelings of stress in a stressful world?

You can respond to the challenges life constantly brings by being calm, clear-headed, and by recognizing that unexpected problems will happen. We all navigate the same road with the same conditions of adversity. If you can stay cool and steer around obstacles, then keep getting back on course, you can survive the difficulties and reach your goals. You cannot avoid stressors, but you can learn how to feel less stressed by them.

Attitude is how you carry yourself through life.

Are you a happy person?

Do others want to be around you or do they turn the other way when they see you coming?

Do you feel lonely?

Are you easily frustrated?

Are you frequently sad, angry, or jealous?

Are you easily annoyed by others?

Does your attitude lift you up through life or does it bring you down?

Do you love what you do for a living?

These are important questions to ask. There is an intimate connection among your mental outlook, your nervous system, and your overall health, particularly your immune system.

Your nervous system and your immune cells communicate with each other every second of the day. It's your responsibility to bring them together in positive alignment. This may sound like no easy task. Positively connecting your mind with your immune system takes regular discipline, and it can be a challenging ***one little thing*** to do.

As you improve your attitude, you will improve your direction over time. Even if you're the happiest person you know, there will always be room for more happiness.

Let us look at ***one little thing*** you can do for 120 days that will turn a good day into a GREAT day. If you practice this

one little thing, it will bring a peace to your life that will make it easier to stay on your path.

Sleep your cares away.

When it comes to attitude, the most important thing is sleep. It seems so simple, but millions of people are falling asleep at the wheel of life because they don't sleep enough in their beds at night. They are tired. They're short-tempered. They're easily frustrated. They're inefficient, making frequent mistakes.

Most people think that adding caffeinated beverages or energy drinks to their day will make them alert so they can work faster. But it just temporarily revs up the engine, spiking blood sugar and overworking adrenal glands. Then your energy crashes down even lower. That engine will eventually burn out and adrenal exhaustion, thyroid disease, or cardiovascular impairment may result. It also raises cortisol levels, causing inflammation through your whole body and making you age more quickly. Caffeine is a short-term fix that takes a heavy toll on your body.

Remember, the ***one little thing*** process is not about giving up, but about adding to your life. Don't worry—I'm not asking you to give up your coffee. Feeling deprived makes it difficult to stick with a healthy routine. This process will make health-depleting habits fall away naturally as you feel more authentically energetic. If you ultimately feel caffeine doesn't give you the sustaining vitality you want, you can minimize caffeine withdrawal symptoms by slowly weaning off this stimulant. But first we will look at an easier, more pleasant ***one little thing*** you can change and really enjoy doing.

Sleep your way to a calmer life.

Sleep is an oasis, a respite from the demands of life. We all, at times, ache for more sleep. But sleep is the easiest place to steal some time from to complete our many responsibilities. But in truth, the less we sleep, the less we accomplish and the more difficult every part of our life becomes.

It's much more difficult to maintain a positive mental attitude with yourself and with others when you're suffering from sleep deprivation.

These are some of the benefits of getting a full night's rest:

- ➔ Improves memory
- ➔ Lengthens attention span
- ➔ Improves and stabilizes mood swings
- ➔ Increases mental alertness

- Increases one's ability to focus
- Human Growth Hormone is secreted for health restoration
- Improves mental and physical healing

TRY THIS:

Focus your attention on getting to sleep every night at a time that will give you at least seven hours of sleep. Some people need eight hours, but if you consistently fall short in this area, start by programming a realistic destination. If you know that your eyes pop open at 5 a.m. every morning, lay your head down on your pillow no later than 10 p.m.

Try this for 120 days. You might be pleasantly surprised.

This is going to take some discipline because there are so many things you can be doing at night when you finally have a few hours to yourself, like painting your nails, catching up with work or email, cruising Facebook, doing laundry, working on that airplane model, cleaning your windows, or organizing your junk drawer. Let it go. Getting enough sleep so you are clear and calm for tomorrow is more important than emails, chores, hobbies, or social media.

Getting to bed at a reasonable hour is a sign of self-respect. Honor your nervous system. Be kind to your body. The sleep you give yourself will pay you back with more efficiency and focus throughout the next day.

Now that you have the sleep thing down, you might be ready to take on another ***one little thing***...or NOT. Remember, this journey belongs to you. You are in complete control of your destination.

TRY THIS:

One of the most important skills you can acquire along the journey is the desire and ability to pay attention to life around you. The ***one little thing*** that can bring you to this place is practicing a discipline called mindfulness.

Mindfulness means paying attention in the moment, or being in the NOW. Many productive members of society hurry through life without paying attention to the details they think of as "unimportant."

Pay attention to the empty space in the room, the gaps between words, and time between tasks. Observe what is not being said in a conversation, to the silence in the room, and to the emptiness that you see in your office, your home, nature, and the universe. When you wash the dishes, really look at the dish, at your hands. Be in the moment. When you talk to your children, look in their eyes, and listen closely to what they're saying. When you work in your garden or walk outside, smell the air, listen to the birds, and drink in the moment with all of your senses.

Master the practice of mindfulness and use this skill as you live life. I promise you that your entire life will change forever.

Apply mindfulness to everything you do during the day, such as spending time with your kids or people you care about, your life at work, playful activities, outdoor fun, eating, and just being alone in a moment wherever you are. Just do this ***one little thing***.

It's not important with what activity you apply the mindfulness concept, but the consistency of the effort. Practicing mindfulness with food that you eat is a great place to start, but you can benefit from using it in any area of your life, such as while relating to another person, sitting in nature, or experiencing the beauty of art.

TRY THIS:

Here is an exercise that you can do every day for 120 days:

Hold a raisin or similar food substance in your hand. Stare at it while you move it around in your fingers, looking at the cracks and crevices on its surface. Squish it between your fingers and feel its plumpness. Pay attention to its color, size, and texture. When you feel connected to the raisin in a way that might make you feel weird or strange, put it in your mouth but do not bite down on it. Roll the raisin around in your mouth, feeling the grooves with your tongue, paying attention to how it rolls around on your cheeks and the roof of your mouth. You may even extract a tiny bit of flavor by this time. The raisin may begin to get soft and squishy as you roll it around and it mixes with your saliva. Pay attention to every detail.

When you feel even more connected to your raisin, and are getting to the place where you are noticing a boredom setting in, bite down on the raisin. Notice how soft or firm it is. Notice how it pulverizes with the chewing process. The most striking thing you'll notice is the explosion of flavor from that little raisin. It's a flavor that you have never experienced from a raisin before. Just be present with it. Experience it. Enjoy every second of it, every calorie, and every sensation from it. Chew it up into a pulpy mass and eventually swallow it when you feel complete and ready to digest it. Feel the mush going down your throat and esophagus. Notice the residue or tiny pieces of raisin left behind in your teeth and between your cheeks. Pay attention to everything.

When you feel like the process is complete, sit quietly in time and space and experience stillness.

After four months of practicing mindfulness, you might be ready for another ***one little thing***...or NOT. This is for you to decide. You are in complete control of your GPS programming all the way through.

You cannot receive more of what you want in life unless you are truly grateful for what you already have.

It's difficult to be grateful when you're in a bad mood. You cannot be in a bad mood when your heart is filled with gratitude because love and gratitude are synonymous.

If you choose to adopt another ***one little thing*** into your attitude about life, make it the attitude of gratitude. You get to decide if you want to bring more love and good feelings into your life. It's your call. If you practice the attitude of gratitude every day for 120 days, your life will change in ways that you never thought possible.

Richard and Vanessa were married for eight years before experiencing difficulties in their relationship. Richard focused on Vanessa's constant negativity about seemingly unimportant things, and Vanessa focused on Richard's emotional unavailability. They often bickered in private and in public, but they loved each other and wanted to resolve their mutual frustrations.

One day, after feeling exhausted by the stress of their animosity, they decided to practice a mental exercise of keeping a gratitude journal about each other for 120 days. Richard bought Vanessa a beautiful red silk journal and Vanessa bought Richard a leather-bound journal. The exercise required them to record in the journal something that they noticed about their partner that they were grateful for every day, no matter how busy they were.

Richard began to notice how Vanessa took time to clean their home, how she kissed him every night before falling asleep, how she made his lunch every day, and how she lovingly cared for their children. He was moved by her thoughtfulness and loving personality. After two weeks into the exercise, Vanessa's negativity seemed to melt away and Richard's love for his wife grew stronger.

Vanessa noticed, soon after beginning the exercise, that Richard was coming home after work to be with her and their children, and she felt grateful for that. She admired how Richard offered to bring the children to the park on a weekend when she was feeling tired. After several weeks of paying attention to everything that she was grateful for in Richard, she began to feel more loved and adored by him, and was no longer feeling emotionally distant from him.

Through the process of bringing forth feelings of gratitude, Richard and Vanessa transformed their relationship into a strong, loving union. They were elated by the amount of progress they had made in only 120 short days.

Keeping a gratitude journal is a powerful way to identify and even create feelings of gratitude that you never knew existed. Feeling and expressing gratitude can make friends out of enemies. It can open up new windows of opportunity, and it can save relationships.

Gratitude will allow you to attract more of what you want into your life by aligning your feelings with your desires. Gratitude toward others will cause them to respond favorably to you, making life just a little bit easier. Whenever people do something nice for you, tell them how grateful you feel and tell them specifically what you appreciate about them and what they have done. Tell your spouse, your children, your partner, or your parent that you love them. Mail, email, Facebook, tweet, or text random messages of gratitude to special people in your life for no reason other than you appreciate them.

TRY THIS:

Here is an exercise that you can do every day for 120 days:

Write down on a piece of paper 10 things that you are grateful for and post the list near your bed. Every morning when you wake up, before you touch your feet to the floor, read these 10 things.

While you're reviewing those 10 things, feel gratitude while creating an image of each of them in your mind. Feel the feelings associated with each blessing you're grateful for.

If you're naming your children, picture your daughter's sweet face in your mind and love her in your heart.

If you're grateful for your job, create an image in your mind of something about it that you love to do, the people you work with, or any aspect of the work that makes you feel happy or fulfilled.

If you're grateful for your partner, picture him in your mind and love him in your heart. Smile. Radiate. Open your heart. Bask in the feelings.

Find your calm center in a stressful world.

Daily responsibilities and unexpected emergencies will always cause stress in your life. But you can greatly improve your ability to meet these challenges with a calm, capable mindset by just changing ***one little thing*** at a time. The changes may feel subtle at first, but I assure you the changes will happen. It's like praying between the lines by absorbing and drinking in the blessings in your life.

Your attitude and how you carry yourself through your day will set your course during times of peace or adversity.

When mindfulness and gratitude become a regular part of your day, it will be easier for you to steer toward peace, even when life gets tough.

CHAPTER FOUR

Just add water.

Nutrition

Our parents handed their eating habits down to us. Some of us may have learned specific nutrition lessons. Others may have just eaten the same foods our parents considered normal without any attention paid to how the food helped or hurt our bodies.

We all know what we like to eat, and what we consider normal to eat. But you run the probability of developing the same diseases that your parents and grandparents had if you share habits that deplete your body.

Through the media and grocery stores, food manufacturers make certain foods seem normal to us, but realize that those are money-driven industries. They don't necessarily look out for your best interest. They want to sell what they can make cheaply and get customers addicted to coming back again and again. Poor food choices add to the risk of more inflammation and health deterioration. The solution is complex. Your body will work better and for longer if you add positive foods and remove negative foods.

Remember that the objective of the ***one little thing*** program is to learn how to improve your outcome by adding, not necessarily taking things away, in the early stages of change. The principles in this book are not based on deprivation, but on adding ***one little thing*** at a time to your life. I do not want to take simple pleasures from you. You will decide if you want to hold on to negative habits. You are in control.

By adding one positive habit at a time, you'll naturally begin to crowd out your health-depleting habits with health-promoting habits. You'll crave the food that makes your body and mood feel better and more energetic. You'll make the shift. This may take time and patience. After all, Rome wasn't built in a day. Your body regenerates every four months. This is the magic of 120 days.

Drink your way to health.

When it comes to nutrition, the most important and logical ***one little thing*** to add to your life is WATER. You cannot live more than a few days without water. That tells you how vital it is to your life and health.

Pure, clean, filtered water can be the difference between weight loss and weight gain, a cloudy mind and clarity, or inflammation and pain-free living. Adding this one small thing can move you to the healthy side of the ledger.

Water hydrates every cell in your body, and it keeps the kidneys active and functional. Water moves waste materials from your bloodstream and your intestines. It keeps your brain functioning. It allows every system in your body to do what it's designed to do, which is to help you reach your highest human potential. Water matters. It's your choice to drink your coffee, your alcohol, and your sugar drinks. Just drink lots of WATER, too.

TRY THIS:

Before taking on hydration as your first ***one little thing*** in the area of nutrition, you'll need to learn how to determine the proper amount of water to take in every day.

Get on a scale and determine your weight in pounds. You may have to borrow a neighbor's scale since you threw yours out the window three chapters ago. Now, take the number you weigh in pounds and cut that number in half. For example, if you weigh 160 pounds, half of that is 80. Then you would aim for drinking 80 ounces of pure water every day.

Once you determine what your number is, your next decision is based upon how you'll be drinking it, either in 8-ounce glasses, 12-ounce bottles, or by random trips to the drinking fountain, which is time-consuming, but could help you get in more walking steps per day. It's your choice.

The rest of the equation is simply a math problem. For example, if you're drinking 8-ounce glasses of water, you'll divide 80 by 8, getting 10. So you would drink 10 glasses of water a day.

Add two more glasses a day if you want to lose weight. Add one more glass of water for every alcoholic, caffeinated, or sugar beverage you consume in a day, because these beverages draw water out of the body. Add two more glasses if you exercised that day. Add another one to two glasses if it's a hot day, or you're perspiring for any reason. If you add these variables to your day, it's conceivable that you may need to drink 20 glasses of water on any given day.

You can see how much water is required every day. If you feel bored by the "nothingness" taste of water, spice it up with just a splash of citrus or natural fruity flavor. Make WATER your ***one little thing*** to get you started down the healing path. Try this for 120 days, but don't add anything else. I know you want to, but resist the temptation.

If you find that you're running to the bathroom too often, and it interferes with your job performance or your life, RECALCULATE ROUTE!

If your calculation requires you to drink eight glasses of water, and you were only drinking three glasses a day, make the decision to drink five glasses a day and work your way up from there. You'll eventually adjust to drinking more water.

You may find that adding more water to your life is a "moving" experience. A happy colon is a happy life.

Be patient. Be kind and gentle with yourself. You have 120 days to create the water habit. Go for it!

When you've successfully added the water habit to your life, it may be time to look at food as your next ***one little thing***, or not...you are in charge of your journey. Your journey might feel complete simply by transforming into a water junkie. This would be a very healthy change that will help your body and mood in many ways.

Why does food matter so much?

Relax. Trust the process. Let's take a peek at the food thing and see what all of the fuss is about.

Nutrition means nourishing yourself. This means physical nourishment, as well as emotional and spiritual nourishment. Nutrition means metabolizing food to give your body energy to survive and take action.

Unfortunately, converting food into energy your body can use causes oxidative stress, which contributes to just about every disease known to man.

Good nutrition involves volume, variety, longevity, and consistently eating foods grown from the ground, trees, or vines, including sea vegetables. These foods decrease inflammation and slow down the aging process by keeping your body chemistry closer to alkaline than acidic.

Eating stresses your body.

To understand what digesting food does to your body, you need to learn about oxidative stress.

Once you understand how eating produces oxidative stress that can hurt you, you can then choose whether you want to take on another ***one little thing***...or not. It's your choice.

When you understand oxidation, you'll see the power in choosing to nourish yourself properly and efficiently.

When heat ignites with oxygen and wood, a fire burns. This burning is oxidation that forms smoke, soot, and ash. These are no good to anyone unless a person is stranded on a deserted island and is desperately trying to signal a rescue plane.

When gasoline mixes with oxygen, it produces horsepower to fuel an engine. The byproduct of this oxidation is carbon monoxide, a poisonous gas that can bring down any human if it is inhaled in high enough concentrations.

When an apple is cut open and the nutrients are exposed to oxygen, the apple turns brown, and kids toss it in the trash in the lunch room.

If you wait too long to fry up latkes after grating the potatoes and making the batter, the whole mess oxidizes and turns brown and mushy, but nobody will complain because they all appreciate how much work goes into making latkes.

The bottom line is that oxidation creates some negative byproducts. So what happens when you digest food?

Turning food into energy damages your body.

You eat food. The food passes through the gastrointestinal tract as you digest it and break it down into molecules your body can use to keep you alive. This energy, or ATP, is produced in the mitochondrion. I call this structure the "battery" of the cell.

Food molecules go through the chemical process to produce energy in the mitochondria. Just like your car puts out toxic carbon monoxide when it oxidizes gas, your cells give off an infinite number of unstable electrons called free radicals. Free radicals hurt your body. These electrons work like sparks that seek and destroy molecules, cells, tissue, and eventually organs and entire body systems.

Every cell in your body takes more than 10,000 free radical hits because free radicals fiddle with the atoms in your cells as they look for an electron partner. Electrons are more stable when they travel in pairs, just like humans. When free radicals damage the body, it's called oxidative stress.

Oxidative stress is synonymous with aging, disease, and eventually death. Don't let this alarm you. This is as natural as a ripened leaf falling off its branch in autumn, or a piece of fruit falling from the tree when it can no longer carry its own weight on the tree. Oxidation is a natural process, but the good news is that we can control the rate of our own oxidative process, allowing our leaves and fruit to stay on our tree a little while longer while we enjoy them and use them.

Free radical electron sparks are destructive. When free radical sparks hit our joint tissue, we develop arthritis inflammation and pain. The entire immune system is vulnerable to free radical damage. It can eventually affect allergy symptoms, colds, flus, and cancer cell growth. DNA, our genetic coding and the blueprint for how every cell replicates, is susceptible to free radical hits, causing a forbidden clone of abnormal cells, called cancer. Free radical hits to the skin from radiation and sun exposure can cause wrinkles, freckles, and dehydration.

Even athletes suffer the effects of oxidation.

As more oxygen is pumped through respiration and moves through the chemical process, there is more potential for a higher oxidative stress level, which can damage even more cells. Athletes breathe in more oxygen and have a higher energy output. Their fireplace is burning more wood at higher temperatures, increasing their oxidative stress levels.

We see an enormous amount of oxidative stress damage in athletes simply because free radical hits cause inflammation in the body and damage cells faster than the body can repair this damage. We call these sports injuries repetitive strain injuries, stress fractures, tendonitis, and overuse injuries. However, oxidative damage in athletes doesn't just occur in the musculoskeletal system, but all over the body. The more free radicals produced through the metabolic process, the more free radical hits the body takes all over, causing the body to age more rapidly.

Once you understand the concept of oxidative damage, you can begin to understand how to slow it down, and your body can start repairing itself. Free radicals need an electron partner to become more stable in the body.

Eat the rainbow.

Electrons in the form of antioxidants (or, "against oxidation") live in colorful plant foods that come from the ground or sea. When we eat large amounts of colorful foods of the rainbow pulled from the ground or picked from a tree or vine, their antioxidants work together to donate their electrons to the volatile and destructive free radicals. This has an overall effect of reducing oxidation and slowing down the aging process in the body. Freshly grown food can minimize the oxidation process. It slows down aging and makes you less susceptible to degenerative disease.

The convenience of processed foods in modern civilization has separated us from living mainly off of fresh, grown food as early man did. Understanding how food ages us more rapidly or slows down the aging process is the knowledge that allows you to choose energy-producing, life-sustaining nutrition.

Our culture has lost sight of food as nutrition because of the big business that processed foods and fast foods has become. Television bombards us with images of very tasty-looking food that will badly damage our bodies. Fast-food establishments have become skilled at attracting customers to their restaurants by offering inexpensive food, play structures, and giveaway toys.

I hope more people will understand oxidative stress and the devastating toll this process takes on your body. Start putting more produce into your diet. Not only do the U.S. Department of Agriculture, the American Heart Association, and the American Cancer Society recommend that we eat 7-13 servings of fresh fruits and vegetables every day, but doing so just might save your life. This may be your next ***one little thing***...or NOT. You are in control of the ride.

You can make adding freshly grown foods your next little change in small ways, if that seems easier and more natural. I will include some simple, easy ways to do this at the end of the chapter.

I know that changing your diet can seem like an overwhelming step that you nag yourself to do, but find yourself avoiding. That's fine. This is your journey. It's your choice to add any new ***one little thing*** to your life.

If you're not ready to make the commitment to add ground foods to your life just yet, consider the idea of making whole food concentrates part of your life.

As a holistic public health nurse, I'm constantly in search of small, inexpensive, and easy-to-master things that can make enormous improvements in a person's health. Supplementation is one of those things. There is a logical process that you can follow to choose the best supplement for you.

Look for two things when searching for a supplement. The first is a whole food supplement. There are many choices of supplements. One choice is whether to eat your supplements in isolated form or whole form.

An isolated nutrient is not natural.

Whole food supplementation is different from an isolated nutrient formula, such as a multivitamin, because it's made from concentrated juice powders of foods. The nutrients are delivered in full synergy with thousands of other nutrients found in the whole food.

After nearly a century of research, the scientific literature is clear and compelling. When a nutrient is separated from the other tens of thousands of chemicals found in unprocessed food, and mega-dosed at high levels in an attempt for the body to recognize that nutrient, it doesn't have the same effect on the body as if the nutrient were ingested in whole food form. Isolated vitamins, minerals, and other nutrients have been shown to negatively affect high-risk individuals.[14] The second thing to do when searching for a nutritional supplement is to look at the scientific evidence, based on the work of credible, third-party researchers. When researchers give a formula to people, you want to see positive changes occur to specific measures of health or characteristics of the body.

When people eat a supplement formula, do good things happen in their bodies? Research should prove bio-availability. This means that the nutrients absorb into the bloodstream. You also want to see evidence of a reduction of oxidative stress throughout the body. This is what foods grown from the ground do for us when we eat them. You want your supplement to do the same thing. I recommend checking at least three well-designed, independent studies confirming these findings. Also, make sure a supplement is safe before you take it or recommend it to others.

My favorite everyday, forever supplement is Juice Plus+ because of the depth of a growing collection of independent research that confirms its safety and effectiveness when people take it.[15] If you can't see the research on a supplement, you'll have to depend on blind faith. Blind faith is like the mystery shortcut when it comes to saving time on your destination. You could very easily get lost and fall further behind. Don't follow an uncharted road when it comes to selecting something that you'll eat every day for the rest of your life.

TRY THIS:

As a community, we aren't experiencing specific nutrient deficiencies, but we are suffering from a deficiency of whole foods. Choose a whole food supplement that makes sense to you, take it consistently every single day for 120 days, and feel the magic. If you don't feel different after taking a supplement for 120 days, try not to feel discouraged, because you may not feel prevention working. Supplementation is not something that you waffle in and out of taking. Do your research, choose the right one for you, and take it consistently for life.

Mary, the woman you learned about in Chapter One who had the diagnosis of MS, decided to make whole food supplementation her first ***one little thing*** of choice. This choice worked well for her because this ***one little thing*** created a cascade of changes that allowed her to organically remove other health-depleting habits from her life without her feeling the losses.

Now that we have your supplementation figured out, are you ready to take the next step? Remember, there is an entire world of health-depleting foods out there that you would be much better off eliminating right now, but that's not what this process is about. We'll focus on adding ***one little thing*** at a time for positive results.

TRY THIS:

Consider making your next ***one little thing*** the habit of adding two servings of green vegetables to your day. No, I'm not kidding. I'm as serious as a heart attack about this one.

One serving of a chopped-up green, leafy vegetable will measure one-half cup. A serving of other whole vegetables will fit in the palm of your hand. Examples of green vegetables include all leaf vegetables such as spinach, red-leaf or romaine lettuce, kale, collards, turnip greens, mustard greens, Swiss chard, zucchini, Brussels sprouts, cabbage, broccoli, green beans, snow peas, organic edamame soy beans, and peas.

Iceberg lettuce does NOT count. It contains fiber and carbohydrates, but not enough nutrients to make a difference.

If you keep in mind that the darker your vegetable's color, the more nutrients are present, you can easily make good decisions as you travel this critical journey.

One of my favorite tricks for adding green vegetables to my day is to make a daily smoothie with a plant protein source, a plant-based milk alternative liquid, ground flax seeds, and fresh fruit. Once you have your smoothie routine down, you can begin to add green, leafy vegetables to the mix, such as kale, green tea, or spinach leaves. You won't know they're in your drink, especially if you're blending berries, as they tend to hide the color and the taste of everything else in the smoothie.

If you haven't been eating vegetables, there is probably a good reason for this. Do you despise the taste of them? Perhaps you don't like to prepare food. Is the availability of vegetables sparse where you live? You might consider researching the area where you live for a service that delivers organically and locally grown produce to your door. This is a great opportunity for you to create customized boxes of fresh produce that you will want to eat.

Consider growing your own vegetables with a traditional garden or on a vertical Tower Garden™ that grows in a small space on your patio or on your balcony.[16]

Whatever your reasons for not eating vegetables, you can do things to change this. Buy a cookbook or download recipes from the Internet that feature vegetable side dishes. Find a good grocery store near you that will serve as a source of healthy, flash-frozen packaged foods. You can experiment to come up with a plan of how to move them into your life and keep them there...or NOT. The journey is yours to experience.

The suggestion to add more green vegetables to your life is based on solid science, but you are in control of your life. You can decide if you want to take this on or continue to live life as you always have.

If you always do what you've always done, you will always get what you always got!

One thing is certain: If you continue to do the same thing as you've always done, you will always be, look, and feel the same. The time clock WILL work against you, and so will all of the food you eat that doesn't contain antioxidants to counter the oxidation of metabolism.

Counting calories never works, so don't even go there.

Instead of counting calories, make your calories count!

Eat foods from the ground that contain a high concentration of nutrients. After all, tomorrow your body will become what you're eating today. I prefer this statement to "You are what you eat." When I hear that statement, I imagine little kids walking around as giant hot dogs and round, giant donuts.

Always remember to be patient with the process and to be gentle with yourself.

CHAPTER FIVE

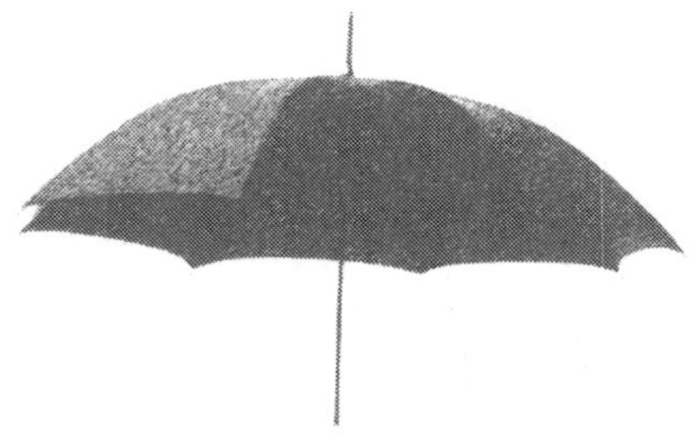

To bring the sun out again when it rains, first make it pour.

The JOLT

Choose ***one little thing*** to improve your life. When you decide on your ***one little thing***, please don't feel like it's etched in stone and handed down to Moses. Look at your journey as a trail with infinite choices simply floating in space. Choices are based on education and trial and error. Your choices should remain interchangeable and flexible.

The important thing is to recognize when the path you're on won't get you to your destination.

RECALCULATE ROUTE!

It may require several turns and even missed turns. Be willing to make a change.

Don't be afraid to fail your way to success.

It may take ten failures before you see the kind of success that makes the difference for you. If ***one little thing*** doesn't work for you, try another ***one little thing***. It doesn't mean that you're a failure. It simply means that you're RECALCULATING ROUTE and taking one step closer to your success. The "failures" are what cause you to feel emotional anguish, but the same failures will eventually allow you to feel accomplished and successful. They are all important. They are all part of your journey.

You WILL relapse.

You WILL become frustrated by not staying on course.

You WILL feel like beating yourself up at some point along the way.

Before you relegate yourself to the land of the lost losers (perhaps once again), consider an alternative way of experiencing your disgust.

Unfortunately, self-loathing behavior is normal and common during the process of making positive changes to your health. If you don't feel this way from time to time, congratulations. You're either in denial or are the rarest of exceptions.

As you begin your self-deprecating journey into the dark side, identify how you feel. Observing the scenery as you travel is part of your journey of self-discovery.

Don't do anything with these feelings. Simply identify them. Are you feeling sad? Are you feeling angry? Are you experiencing shame, apathy, or desperation? Observe the feeling. Don't worry about doing anything with it—just recognize it for now.

Once again, I'm not interested in submerging you under a sea of deprivation. I'm not even going to try to force you out of this desperate place. I wouldn't dream of taking your self-abusive behavior from you. You are exactly where you need to be, and your journey is perfectly designed, including the self-abuse. This is part of your process. Relax. Breathe. Accept it. When you are ready, RECALCULATE ROUTE.

Now is a good time to define some of this self-loathing language. You're already thinking it, so you might as well deal with it consciously. Allow me to help you through this step. Simply fill in the blanks with your name and you will be on your way to self-discovery.

"____________, you are the biggest loser on the planet."

"You can never complete anything, ________________."

"For Pete's sake, ________________, why do you continually put yourself through this torture?"

"I should have never started doing this. I knew I wouldn't be able to do this."

"What a loser."

"Really…?"

"Am I for real?"

"What kind of example am I setting for my kids who are watching me?"

"My spouse thinks I'm a loser, too."

Go to the dark side and stay there for as long as you'd like—a day, a week, a year if you need to.

Now that you're fully present on the dark side of your self-destructive process, it might be helpful to write down your own personal phrase that you like to use:

DO NOT SKIP THIS STEP. It is critical to your process. Go back to the blank space now and put your own words on the page. Be in control of your own flogging.

Time has passed. Was it an hour? Was it a day, a week, or a year?

Who cares?

Let's move on. You need a JOLT!

If you think that the storm has passed, and you feel somewhat emotionally drained, you might be ready to move forward and consider taking the next three steps.

STEP 1: Create your defining moment for RECALCULATING ROUTE. Decide that it is time.

STEP 2: Go back to Chapter One and identify your "why." You decided it was time to make a change. Be sure to connect with the emotion behind your "why."

Has your "why" changed between the time you started reading the book and now? If you put deep thought into creating your "why" in Chapter One, a drastic change in your "why" is unlikely. If it has changed, rewrite your "why" and bookmark the page for quick reference when you start beating yourself up again.

J-O-L-T is my acronym for just-one-little-thing. This is a book about doing only one thing at a time to achieve successful results.

STEP 3: Go back to your ***one little thing***. . .

Start over if you have to, but please start only ***one little thing***.

Do NOT try to make up for lost time by doing two or three little things.

The following words mean "ONE" in six different languages!

ONE EIN UNO ICHI EEN UN

Life contains an infinite series of choices. You can make choices that burn out your engine and cause you to spit and sputter down the road, or you can make choices that turn you into a champion.

It's my hope that you choose to move your body in a way that builds strength and stamina, so that when life gets tough you can continue to travel your personal journey with confidence.

It's my wish that you positively align your attitude with your immune system to give you the strength and will to fight cancer and other debilitating diseases.

It's my prayer that you choose to nourish your body with an abundance of plant foods to maximize your life-sustaining energy and live life to your full potential.

Begin today. Just try ***one little thing***.

Or not.

It's your choice.

You can begin your journey now, and when you find you have stepped off course, just RECALCULATE ROUTE.

References

1. Center for Disease Control, June 2010; National Center for Health Statistics. Source: Prevalence of Overweight, Obesity, and Extreme Obesity Among Adults, United States, Trends 1960-1962 through 2007-2008 by Cynthia L. Ogden, Ph.D., and Margaret D. Carroll, S.S.P.H., Division of Health and Nutrition Examination Surveys.

2. Center for Disease Control, December 2010; National Center for Health statistics, Vital Health Stat 10(249), 2010. Source: Summary Health Statistics for U.S. Adults: National Health Interview Survey, 2009. By Pleis JR, Ward BW, Lucas JW.

3. Center for Disease Control 2011; National Center for Chronic Disease Prevention and Health Promotion. Source: 2011 National Diabetes Fact Sheet.

4. Center for Disease Control, July 2010. Source: National Center for Disease Prevention and Health Promotion, Division for Heart Disease and Stroke Prevention.

5. Center for Disease Control, December 2010; National Center for Health statistics, Vital Health Stat 10(249), 2010. Source: Summary Health Statistics for U.S. Adults: National Health Interview Survey, 2009. By Pleis JR, Ward BW, Lucas JW.

6. American Psychological Association; Stress in America. 2011. http://www.apa.org/news/press/releases/stress/2011/impact.aspx

7. American Psychological Association; Stress in America. 2011. http://www.apa.org/news/press/releases/stress/2011/impact.aspx

8. Adamson, Eve. The Everything Stress Management Book: Practical Ways to Relax, Be Healthy, and Maintain Your Sanity. 2001. http://www.ourstressfullives.com/stress-statistics.html

9. American Psychological Association; Stress in America. 2011. http://www.apa.org/news/press/releases/stress/2011/impact.aspx

10. American Psychological Association; Stress in America. 2011. http://www.apa.org/news/press/releases/stress/2011/impact.aspx

11. American Psychological Association; Stress in America. 2011. http://www.apa.org/news/press/releases/stress/2011/impact.aspx

12. American Psychological Association; Stress in America. 2008. http://www.apa.org/news/press/releases/2008/10/stress-in-america.pdf

13. America's State of Mind: A Report by MedCo. 2011. http://medco.mediaroom.com/

14. Carotene and Retinol Efficacy Trial (CARET study), performed by researchers at Fred Hutchison Cancer Research Center in Seattle, WA. http://www.compass.fhcrc.org/caretweb/

15. http://www.JuicePlus.com

16. http://TowerGarden.com

Made in the USA
Charleston, SC
25 March 2012